GRIMOIRE

OF

MAGICK

GRIMOIRE OF MAGICK

GRIMOIRE OF MAGICK

© 2019 ALEISTER NACHT

PUBLISHED BY LOKI / SPECKBOHNE PUBLISHING

ISBN-10: 0-9903693-7-4
ISBN-13: 978-0-9903693-7-0

HARDCOVER EDITION FIRST PRINT
10 9 8 7 6 5 4 3 2 1

UNITED STATES OF AMERICA

GRIMOIRE OF MAGICK

BOOK _____ OF _____

Topics To Consider Recording
Before / During the Event

- PLANNING
- MOON PHASE / DATE / HOUR
- SABBAT / ESBAT / EQUINOX / SOLSTICE
- PURIFICATION / BANISHING / GROUNDING
- CASTER / PRIEST / PRIESTESS
- NAME OF EVENT: RITUAL / RITE / SPELL / CURSE / HEX / INCANTATION / INVOCATION / EVOCATION / CONVOCATION / LUCID DREAM / ASTRAL NATURE / ENERGY BUILDING AND MANIPULATION / MASTEMA / ELEMENTAL / CEREMONIAL
- DESCRIPTION OF EVENT
- PURPOSE / OBJECTIVES / SCOPE OF EVENT
- SOLE / COVEN / PARTICIPANTS
- ROBE / SKYCLAD
- ELIXIR / POTIONS / OILS / HERBS / INCENSE
- CHAKRAS - PHYSICAL, METAPHYSICAL, KUNDALINI, COLORS, SYNCHRONICITY
- TALISMAN / AMULET / CRYSTALS / GEMSTONES
- SIGIL / SYMBOLS / THEBAN / ENOCHIAN
- MEDITATION / MANTRA / ESOTERIC CHANT / SINISTER CHANT / SCRYING
- DEITIES TO INVOKE
- TEMPLE, ALTAR ORIENTATION, & IMPLEMENTS

AFTER THE EVENT

- DURATION OF EVENT
- RESULTS / EFFECTIVENESS OF EVENT
- RECEIVED MYSTERY / ENLIGHTENMENT / GNOSIS / SELF-ACTUALIZATION
- PARADOX DIMENSION INTERACTIONS
- ASTRAL NATURE EVENTS
- IMMEDIATE FEELINGS, IMAGES, EFFECTS, AND AURA
- DEITY MANIFESTATION / INTERACTIONS
- DRAWINGS / ILLUSTRATIONS
- FOLLOW-UP ACTIONS
- LESSONS LEARNED FROM EVENT

ENDS

- EAT
- NEST
- DRINK
- SCRIBE

GRIMOIRE OF MAGICK

TABLE OF CONTENTS

X

GRIMOIRE OF MAGICK

GRIMOIRE OF MAGICK

GRIMOIRE OF MAGICK

GRIMOIRE OF MAGICK

xx

GRIMOIRE OF MAGICK

GRIMOIRE OF MAGICK

GRIMOIRE OF MAGICK

GRIMOIRE OF MAGICK

GRIMOIRE OF MAGICK

GRIMOIRE OF MAGICK

GRIMOIRE OF MAGICK

GRIMOIRE OF MAGICK

GRIMOIRE OF MAGICK

GRIMOIRE OF MAGICK

GRIMOIRE OF MAGICK

GRIMOIRE OF MAGICK

GRIMOIRE OF MAGICK

GRIMOIRE OF MAGICK

GRIMOIRE OF MAGICK

GRIMOIRE OF MAGICK

www.ingramcontent.com/pod-product-compliance
Lightning Source LLC
Chambersburg PA
CBHW030519100426
42813CB00001B/88